CHANGING
JARROW

PAUL PERRY

D1341573

FONTHILL

For Jack
my Grandson in Sydney, Australia
and my late parents Lucy & Albert Perry

Whilst every effort has been made to photograph the modern day equivalent
images in this publication from exactly the same viewpoint, it has not always
been possible; therefore the angle of view differs slightly in some cases from that
of the original image.

Fonthill Media Limited
Fonthill Media LLC
www.fonthillmedia.com
office@fonthillmedia.com

First published in the United Kingdom 2014

British Library Cataloguing in Publication Data:
A catalogue record for this book is available from the British Library

ISBN 978-1-78155-275-9

Typeset in 9.5pt on 12pt Mrs Eaves Serif Narrow.
Typesetting by Fonthill Media. Printed in the UK.

INTRODUCTION

Since commencing my own personal collection of photographs of Jarrow and Hebburn in 1966, I have witnessed many changes especially on my own doorstep in Jarrow, and I for one, have to admit some were for the ongoing benefit of the town and its people, and others not so. The mass demolition during the 1960s of some of the fine historic buildings in Jarrow is nothing short of shameful. Many beautiful churches, countless public houses and private residences in and around the town centre were razed to the ground, seemingly under the guise of progress, and without an utterance of the word preservation.

Today we are all collectors of photographs in one form or another, from the adolescents who adorn their bedroom walls with posters and pictures of their favourite singers, film stars or sporting heroes, to proud parents who make snapshot albums of every significant moment of their children's lives.

Photography is everywhere these days; we cannot escape it. If any medium could be said to dominate our cultural lives, surely it must be the photograph, if we are to believe the quotation, each and every one is equivalent to a thousand words which tells it own individual story. We are captivated by photography, which has the power to conjure up simple memories of times gone by, or transport us to the ends of the planet and beyond. Photography, from the Greek word *photo* meaning light and *graphien* meaning to write roughly translated means 'to write with light'. There is evidence of the simple pinhole camera dating from as early as the fourth century. This we can ascertain from Chinese philosopher Mo-Ti and his Greek counterparts Aristotle and Euclid who described them around this time. Very early cameras, such as the camera obscura, were used solely for projecting images as they had no means of recording, making them, little more than elaborate pinhole cameras.

The photograph has become arguably the greatest influence upon our contemporary myths. From the very beginning of its invention around 1838, this medium has been widely discussed, argued about and hailed as one of the greatest achievements of the nineteenth century, and oft times referred to as an offspring of both art and science.

But for many years after its invention the debate goes on, is photography an art? Some photographers declared themselves artists, while others rejected the status; however, it is perhaps one of the major art forms from this period. Then there are others who think photography is not an art at all, quite simply because it is mechanical, as photographers did not need the manual dexterity of other artists such as painters and sculptors. We might marvel and at the same time be sceptical of the combination of skill and vision of photographers gone by, who have enabled us to enjoy today the results of their labour and techniques. But photographs do not have to be significant works of art, they simply can be fascinating cultural artefacts, historical documents or a split second of a loved one, frozen in time.

This volume relies on both the art and science of photography to illustrate Jarrow's Changing Places.

Ferry Street
Lamb's snack food's was founded in 1937 at a small factory in Birtley Co Durham, manufacturing potato crisps. Because of the demand for this popular snack, larger premises were sought and a site at Jarrow was purchased, and by 1949 the building in Ferry Street was converted. The factory was installed with the most up to date machinery, so that in the cooking and packaging the crisps were untouched by hand. The output rose to fifteen times that of the former factory at Birtley. A process was developed at the factory monitoring potato quality, making this one of the most modern efficient plants of the day.

CHANGING
JARROW

Ormonde Street

Ninety Two Ormonde Street was the address of chemist William Penman, this can be verified by Ward's Directory, who produced a chronicle of businesses in towns and villages nationwide. Penman was not only an acknowledged chemist he was also a highly respected town councillor, who served the electorate in the Jarrow ward. The first sitting of the newly formed council was in 1875. It was deemed right and fitting the prominent position of councillor was entrusted to the town's eminent citizens, many of them being local businessmen.

ACKNOWLEDGEMENTS

I am indebted to the following people for their help in the production of this publication.

Terry Kelly & Tim Richardson at the *Shields Gazette*
Anthony Perry
Angela & Oliver Snowden
Joanne Butler
Jean Taylor
Staff at Jarrow Branch Library
Norman Dunn
Peter Maguire
David Morton at the *Newcastle Chronicle & Journal*
John Joyce
Joe Campbell
Lawrence Cuthbert
Les Power
Revd Fr Gerard Martin

Special thanks to my brother Malcolm for his perseverance support and patience, all of which he has in abundance.

Station Stairs

Similar to many other towns which have grown up rapidly, Jarrow had many requirements. One in particular was the need for a footbridge spanning the passenger and mineral railway lines at Jarrow station, linking the north and south sides of the town. In 1844 it was decided to erect a stairway connecting the two points which rapidly and not surprisingly became known as the station stairs. By 1891 plans were being drawn to elaborate upon this simple structure because of the danger it created during inclement weather. Alas, a shortage of funds for the proposed modifications halted its progress. As an alternative, the existing walkway was reinforced enough to support the weight of a roof and a glass sided canopy, and remained this way until it was demolished during the 1970s. A similar structure, the metro bridge evident here in the more modern of the accompanying images, was erected around 1980 for those wishing to access this part of town and beyond.

Bede Industrial Estate

A visit in 1945 of Sir Stafford Cripps MP and President of the Board of Trade was to inject new life into the town with the creation of the Bede Industrial Estate, which attracted many new industries to Jarrow and in turn generated a lot of very welcome business. A variety of small, medium and large factory units became available for the manufacture of a wide range of commodities, from retail goods to raw materials for the chemical, textile, electronic, and tobacco industries among them. Although much of the work was for women, nevertheless, the employment offered was a vital contribution to the town's recovery after the second war. Today more than sixty years after its inauguration, the once vibrant estate is somewhat reduced in size, but remains an integral part of the town's rich industrial heritage.

Ellison Street

This well appointed smart terrace of houses in Ellison Street dates from the second half of the nineteenth century, and was typical of the type of accommodation which people in Northeast England became familiar with. As a consequence, much of the housing in central Jarrow was terraced; similar to the accompanying photograph from 1920. Any building with a gable became ideal for advertising, and a target for the agencies that specialised in this type of promotion. Anything and everything was advertised in this manner, especially local theatre and cinema attractions. The "Kino" cinema advertisement clearly visible in the image was built in Grange Road in 1866 on the site of former slipper baths and washhouses. The cinema later changed its name to The Regal, and then to The Crown before it was demolished in the 1980s.

Grange Road

This part of Jarrow at the junction of Grange Road and Ellison Street has always been busy with people and traffic, but not always for the right reasons. The gathering of unemployed men photographed in the older of these images from 1934, were idling away time, after losing their jobs. The world famous Palmer Shipyard announced its closure the same year. This abrupt closure rendered 10,000 men, women and boys out of work. It was this bitter blow and coupled with the town's unemployment figures, which in 1934 were rising to a staggering 80 per cent, gave birth to the infamous Jarrow Crusade. The building to the left of the older of these two images was Martins Bank, which was later merged into the Barclays group. Other than this the scene remains much as it did eighty years ago.

High Street

This was the site of the Durastic Company in High Street pictured in 1950, where bitumen was manufactured up until the 1960s; it was around this time the company relocated to larger premises in Western Road. Bitumen is a component of the building industry, coupled with roofing felt the marriage ensures a reliable method of waterproofing. The site lay derelict for many years until West Cumberland Farmers constructed a depot with offices. It was from here the company distributed fuel oil for the domestic market. WCS was originally a farmers' co-operative founded in 1911 in Brampton, Cumbria where their head office is situated. The company ceased trading in Jarrow during the 1970s in favour of larger premises at Peterlee in County Durham; they also operate a network of depots in the Midlands. Today the premises are occupied by Expedient Training Services.

Oil Storage Tanks

By 1946 and despite the war years, much had been achieved to improve the recovery of the town. The council wasted no time or effort to attract new industries. Together with the assistance from the Northeast Development Council and the Board of Trade, an oil installation terminal was developed in the east end of the town. The site was chosen as it was in close proximity to the deep water's of the river Tyne and the North Sea. The complex was capable of storing up to 24 million litres of petroleum spirit and fuel oil in its twenty or so enormous storage tanks. Regular deliveries of the flammable liquids were made by rail on a specially constructed mineral line which terminated inside the terminal, and distributed nationally by road via a fleet of articulated lorries. During the late 1950s, a pumping station was erected on the riverside enabling the fuel to arrive by both sea and rail. The vessels discharged their cargo ashore through a network of pressurised pipes. Today, the area forms part of a ring road which bypasses the town centre.

Tyne Street

Many of the town's fifty-four public houses around the time when this photograph was taken during the 1950s, were tied to one brewery The Staith House pictured, was tied to Newcastle Breweries, who later became Scottish & Newcastle Breweries Ltd. The other option was a 'freehouse' status, which allowed the publican the freedom to serve beers from independent brewers. Arrol, Nimmo's and Flowers ales were all available in various outlets around Jarrow, but it was Newcastle Breweries along with Vaux, a Sunderland-based brewery who led the way. Towards the end of this terrace was another public house the Commercial Hotel which was originally a seventeenth century coaching inn. A name change in 1972 to the 'Gaslight' and then later to the 'Tunnel Tavern' and remained so until the building was demolished in 2003, making way for the second Tyne Tunnel. Today the area has been totally transformed and beautifully landscaped, as portrayed in the accompanying image.

Back Ellison Street

The rear of this well-cared-for terrace of houses in Ellison Street is featured here though not necessarily photographed on the same day as the picture on page nine. The smaller shed-like structures in the yards are sculleries, an early type of kitchen with very few amenities including a coal fired oven, this we can ascertain by the smoking chimney. Also contained within the yard were a coalhouse and toilet facilities. When these houses were built in the nineteenth century, coal was delivered through a hatch in the outside wall which was usually adjacent to the ash toilet; ash from the fire grate was used to sanitise the 'middens' as these toilets were referred to prior to cisterns being fitted. Another hatch was located towards the bottom of the outside wall which was used by sanitary men, nicknamed 'midnight marauders' who would shovel away the ash and refuse during the early hours. By the 1950s, the toilets had been fitted with flushing cisterns and the hatch bricked up. A cold water supply was also a feature of the yards. Nothing remains of this terrace today being demolished during the 1950s; in its place are an access road to the bus station and Lifeskills, a company dedicated to providing new skills for the unemployed.

Monkton Coke Works

From 1936 the Jarrow skyline was illuminated by a fiercely burning flame courtesy of the Monkton Coke Works. The coal processing plant was a partial gift from the government as a response to the efforts of the Jarrow Crusade. Was this simply an afterthought by Prime Minister Stanley Baldwin, after his government's abrupt refusal of assistance to the 200 men who marched to the capital for the right to work? Perhaps we will never know, but the decision was very welcome as the plant provided much employment. Coke is a fuel with very few impurities and high carbon content derived from coal. Coke generally, is a naturally hard porous substance, but the commonly used form is usually manmade and when ignited burns almost odourless and without smoke. The burning flame was extinguished in 1990 when the plant closed. The former site is now occupied by Merchant Court, a lucrative business park bringing more revenue to the borough.

Buddle Street

Lamplighters were slowly being phased out at the introduction of electricity to our streets. This happened in Jarrow in 1900 after a meeting at the Corporation Offices to discuss the possibility of electric light to illuminate our streets and homes. As funding the scheme became an issue, alas only the main streets and thoroughfares were to see the benefits of electricity. Gas was to remain the prime source of illumination in our streets, and in our homes for many more years. This charming little photograph of a lamplighter at work was taken in 1953, at the junction of Buddle Street and Commercial Road. Today the scene has changed beyond recognition, in recent years the area was reclaimed for the construction of the second Tyne Tunnel, upon completion in 2010, the former construction site was landscaped.

Grant Street

This quite rare photograph of Gaudies bakery in Grant Street was taken from the station stairs. The property in this part of town was in a poor state of repair and within another ten or so more years, the crumbling buildings were being prepared for demolition as part of a development programme. The Alberta CIU social club building in Albert Road was showing severe signs of decay around the same time, and as the committee sought alternate premises for the club, the recently vacant site Gaudies once occupied seemed perfect. After planning permission was granted, work commenced in 1979. Today the club is a thriving concern and one of the few CIU clubs which remain in the region.

Monkton Level Crossing

The Tyneside region is now peppered with level crossings since the inauguration of the Metro Transit System in 1980. Prior to this, level crossings were usually only seen on mineral lines, where the lines crossed a main road or other thoroughfare, and only operated during the transportation of domestic fuel and flammable liquids. These manually operated gated crossings prevented all manner of traffic from crossing the lines when the arrival of a goods train was imminent. These gates also prevented animals straying on to the highway when the gates were not in use. Automatic barriers came into operation in this country in 1961. This particular line was managed by the National Coal Board which commenced at the Monkton Coke Works, terminating at Jarrow Staiths where the coal laden wagons discharged their cargo to waiting colliers bound for London and beyond. After the demise of the coke works, the line was closed along with this crossing at Monkton Village and others further down the line at Albert Road, and Berkeley Street.

Palmer Memorial Hospital

The Palmer Memorial Hospital was erected in Clayton Street in 1871, by its founder Charles Mark Palmer who in 1851, with his brother George, founded the Palmer shipbuilding empire. The hospital was for the sole use of their faithful workforce. The building was maintained with an annual contribution from the company, and subscriptions from its employees. The hospital was dedicated to Palmer's first wife Jane who had passed away six years previous in 1865. Jane was dedicated to charitable events and to the welfare of the people of Jarrow throughout her married life, and was marked with the erection of a beautiful stained glass window in the main entrance. Alas the aging one-hundred-year-old building was demolished in 1973 and replaced with the NHS hospital we are familiar with today. The stained glass window was carefully removed and replaced within the new hospital which was opened by HRH The Princess Royal in 1987. The Griffin depicted atop the entrance in the older of these two photographs, has also been preserved and resides in a memorial garden within the confines of the hospital.

Walter Street

The Cottage public house was situated at the junction of North Street and Walter Street, nestled between two blocks of high rise flats Ellen Court to the left, and Wilkinson Court, seen here in the older of these two photographs which was taken in November 2000 just prior to its demolition. These apartment blocks were constructed in 1963 and named in memory of the town's most memorable member of parliament Ellen Wilkinson, who was responsible for playing a major role in the organisation of the 'Jarrow Crusade' in 1936. The century old building was purpose built as a public house then called the Forge & Hammer a name synonymous to Jarrow which reflects the town's rich association with an industrial past. The area the former building once occupied is now a resident's car park.

Commercial Road

This fascinating old image from 1904 shows another aspect of track laying for the forthcoming tram service, which commenced two years later in 1906, and operated smoothly and efficiently for thirty-five years, until 1929, at the introduction of the motor bus. The photograph was taken at the junction of Grange Road and Staple Road and shows clearly the tracks progress along Commercial Road. The system operated from the tram sheds in Tyne Dock and terminated in Western Road. Men and boys have had a fascination for construction work it seems since the beginning of time. Laying the seventeen miles of track through our streets attracted many onlookers eager to see its progress. The more modern of these two images shows the scene as it is today, with no evidence whatsoever of the network of rails.

Chapel Road

This lovely little picture of Chapel Road looks towards Ellison Street and shows the gables of the quaint and tiny cottages in Charles Street, Hibernian Road and Caledonian Road in 1953. The spire to the right of the image is that of the Presbyterian Church in Ellison Street which was built in 1869. This was one of the town's ten places of worship which were built around the same time. Sadly only two of which survive today, Christ Church which also dates from 1869, the other St Bede's in Chapel Road, just out of shot in this image, which dates from 1861. Shortly after this photograph was taken the cottages were demolished to make way for the shopping centre, which was reputed to be the first of its kind in the country.

High Street

Although reasonably modern in its appearance this block of maisonettes date from 1953, when the shops were occupied by from left to right Gilhooly's fruit and vegetable shop, Hanlon's grocery, Albert Jones family butcher and Shanahans newsagent. Down the years the businesses changed ownership many times until the building was demolished in 2006, as the area it once occupied was required for the new Tyne Tunnel. The original tunnel was opened in 1967 by HRH Queen Elizabeth II. Her Majesty returned to Jarrow once again in 2012 to officially open the latest Tyne crossing. The modern photograph shows clearly how clever landscaping conceals any evidence of industrial activity.

Church Bank

Jarrow Hall pictured was built between 1785 and 1800 by Simon Temple as his private residence. He was born in 1759 in South Shields, son of wealthy parents who owned a small but successful and prosperous shipbuilding business. In 1795 temple acquired a substantial estate in Jarrow, which included St Paul's church and surrounding area. In 1798 he opened a new dry dock at South Shields, reputed to be one of the most efficient in the country of the day. In 1803, he commenced work on the infamous Alfred Pit at Jarrow creating many jobs. It was Simon Temple who was the godfather of the industrial growth at Jarrow. During the 1950s and '60s, the council used the neglected old house for storage. The hall was restored to its former beauty around 1970 and converted into the Bede Monastery Museum. Today it forms part of the internationally recognised Bede's World, Heritage Centre.

Miners White Cottages

These white walled miners' cottages were built in 1804 by Simon Temple, close to St Paul's church. The caring industrialist provided this accommodation here and in nearby High Street for his workforce who toiled in both his shipyard at Dunkirk Place and the Alfred Pit. Temple's mismanagement, foolhardy mining investments and his many failing business interests resulted in his inevitable bankruptcy. Temple died penniless at the home of his former manservant in 1822 aged sixty-three, a very sad end to an important industrialist who contributed so much to the development of Jarrow. Today there is no evidence whatsoever that this part of Jarrow was ever inhabited.

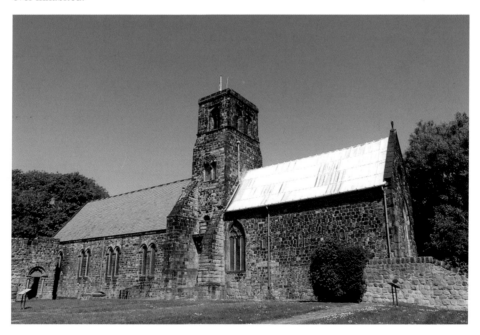

Ferry Landing
From as early as 1837, crossing the River Tyne at Jarrow to a point on the north side was somewhat of an ordeal. This short journey was often made by a sculler boat, the 'scull' being the oar which propelled the boat and gave the simple vessel its direction. From around 1852, the crossings were made in not such a perilous fashion, by a steam powered paddle passenger only ferry. By 1883, the vessel *G H Dexter* was added to the ferry service, again this was used for foot passengers, with the addition of horse drawn carts and hand barrows. The Palmer built vessel was accompanied by another *C M Palmer* which was introduced to the service one year later in 1884. The two over worked vessels were retired in 1923. It was then, the ferry *A B Gowan I* made its debut, and for the first time it was to carry motor vehicles. Some years later *A B Gowan II* was introduced, and remained in service until 1967 and the opening of the Tyne Tunnel. A passenger ferry still operates between North and South Shields.

Arndale Centre

There have been hundreds of photographs taken of the Arndale shopping centre since it was officially opened in 1961 by children's entertainer Harry Corbett and his famous glove puppet 'Sooty'. The accompanying similar images date from 1963, of Viking Precinct and again fifty years later in 2014. The flat roofed 1960s style buildings created many problems for the tenants. Because of these flat roofs, rain water collected and eventually found its way into the premises below, creating much damage. This ongoing problem was rectified by the centre's owners at that time – P&O Properties – with pitched roofs during a total refurbishment programme in the 80s, and at the same time the complex was renamed the Viking Centre. Over the years the rented shop units have changed hands many times, none of the original one hundred businesses from 1961 have survived. F. W. Woolworth, one of the first to take premises in the centre survived the longest, forty-six years until they ceased trading in 2007.

Davy Roll Company

The Davy Roll Company, a local business originated and is based in Gateshead. The company was incorporated in 1920 and supplies the metal working industry with cast rolls and is a subsidiary of the Union Electric Steel Corporation. The Jarrow plant was purchased during the seventies, prior to this and from the early part of the twentieth century it traded under the name of the Jarrow Metal Industry, who also manufactured steel rolls and ingots for industry. During the 1940s and '50s bomb casings were made here for the Ministry of Defence. Virtually every component for the shipbuilding and steel industries were made on the illustrious River Tyne, most of which were for local use but still quite a large percentage were sold to companies both at home and abroad. Today the site is occupied by the Kings Industrial Estate, manufacturing goods but on a much smaller scale.

Mayfield Girls School

In 1928, the parish of St Bede acquired two large houses in Pine Street, for the purpose of converting them into a school for senior girls. Prior to 1928 the girls were educated at a school in Grant Street and when the new school became available the girls were transferred to the newly appointed Mayfield Senior Girls School, subsequently the Grant Street building became an infant school. After a direct hit by an enemy bomb in 1941, the building was devastated and as a consequence, the children were moved to and educated at Mayfield the tired old building was demolished in 1979. Today the former site of the school in Pine Street is now a housing complex and close by a purpose built doctors surgery, aptly named the Mayfield Medical Centre.

Jarrow & Hebburn Co-operative Society Dairy

The Co-operative dairy was built on this site during the recovery years, after the second war in the 1950s and remained the regions main depot for milk distribution up until 1990. During a reshuffle later in the decade around 1993, the ailing dairy was closed along with many more of the Jarrow & Hebburn Co-operative outlets, sadly all of which disappeared from our streets by the end of the decade. The area the dairy once covered was considered a prime location for redevelopment. Barrett Homes bought the site and constructed detached residences which became available in 1996. Today the housing complex Calf Close Drive is now well established and is a desirable place to live.

Cemetery Bank

Plans for a municipal housing estate on waste ground behind Jarrow cemetery were in place as early as 1955, but it wasn't until the mid 1960s when the first of these houses became available on Hill Park Estate. The only accessible route to the estate was via the 'cemetery bank'. Prior to the housing estate being built, this route was used solely for access to the cemetery, but with an increase in traffic levels, and the introduction of a bus service to the estate the road was having to cope with much more traffic than it was originally intended. By the 1980s a bridge spanning the River Don at the foot of the bank was showing severe signs of excess wear and tear, and major remedial work became necessary on the ninety-five-year-old bridge, in the interests of health and safety. The older of these two images shows precisely the extent of the work carried out on the bridge. Today traffic levels have steadily increased but the reinforced bridge will last well into the twenty-first century.

Bede Burn Road

When York Avenue was constructed it was reputed to be the first dual carriageway in the country. Opened in 1928, by HRH the Duchess of York, the avenue swiftly became one of the major roads in and out of town, which eventually saw an increase in traffic, and created problems for resident parking. The 1990s saw the introduction of traffic calming measures which resulted in the avenue being reduced to single carriageway status and with the addition of a lane solely for the use of cyclists. This carve up and narrowing of the lanes created the very welcome parking bays, and at the same time resolving a speeding problem. The pinch pointing commenced at the junction where York Avenue meets Bede Burn Road as seen in the accompanying image, and continued the full length of the tree lined thoroughfare.

Back Monkton Road

As part of the plan for redeveloping the town, the council decided to develop a seven-acre site in the central area for a shopping centre complete with 100 shops, parking for 200 cars and a tenpin bowling centre. The site was chosen as it was conveniently close to both railway and bus stations. In 1955, the area was cleared, making way for the proposed Arndale centre. The properties in Charles Street, Caledonian Road, Hibernian Road and one side of Grange Road had to be demolished. The most economical and efficient way to complete the task was to burn them down. This was entrusted to Durham County Fire Service. The transformation of the area and the construction of the shopping complex are evident in the older of these two images which was taken from Chapel Road in 1959. The remaining shops and houses were demolished very soon after, in keeping with the area. The scene today bears no resemblance whatsoever to the modern day equivalent.

Monkton Road

After twenty or so years, the shopping centre was showing signs of wear and tear and was greatly in need of refurbishment. This photograph of Monkton Road was taken from the former site of the Festival Flats. The derelict building to the left of the image was the Queens Head public house, which was in the process of being demolished around 1986 when the photograph was taken; the site it once occupied became a temporary car park. The immediate foreground and the area to the right of it also became parking facilities eventually the whole area was demolished. Today as witnessed in this modern day equivalent image, this part of the shopping centre and Monkton Road have been totally transformed and the area is now occupied by Morrison's supermarket.

Western Road

Not surprisingly, the Consett Iron Company originated in Consett County Durham in 1864 specialising in the manufacture of iron and steel, but were also active in the mining of limestone. The company was successor to the Derwent Iron Company founded in 1840. In 1924, the company was valued at £3.5 million and wealthy enough to open a plant at Jarrow in 1938, on the former site of the Palmer shipyard after its surprise collapse in 1933. The company managed to continue production during the war years, despite having to use second grade iron ore. The company was nationalised in 1951, into the Iron and Steel Corporation of Great Britain, but denationalised soon after. A further nationalisation happened in 1967 when it became British Steel. The Consett works and the Jarrow plant became unviable to British Steel and as a consequence were mothballed but eventually closed in 1980. The former plant is now a lucrative venture once again as the Viking Industrial Park.

Ellison Street

Jarrow was a bustling and prosperous town with a population of around 30,000 when the older of these two photographs was taken in 1916. Palmer's shipyard's order books were full to capacity and were meeting the demands of their clients from the four corners of the earth. Just visible in the distance we see Palmer's mighty overhead cranes which for eighty plus years dominated the Jarrow skyline. It is difficult to imagine, but in just twenty short years, the town was in dire straits. The closure of Palmer's dealt a devastating blow to the people of Jarrow. Not only did Palmer's close but also many smaller businesses that relied upon the success of the world famous shipyard. In the foreground of the image we see the Longmore Memorial Fountain and horse trough erected here in Ellison Street in 1891, to the memory of Joseph Longmore, who died in 1890, he was the founder member of the Venerable Bede Lodge and sons of Temperance. The fountain was moved from this location to a prime position in Springwell Park. The old horse trough which sat in front of the fountain mysteriously disappeared in 1905 and has never been seen since.

Grange Road

This characterful photograph taken in Grange Road in 1955 showing the town hall and council chambers which is to the right of the photograph. The 1902 building was designed by South Shields architect Fred Rennoldson, the imposing spire of Christ Church in the centre of the photograph, dates from 1869. The town hall clock however, did not appear until 1951, the cost £1,000 was met by the residue of the 'Surrey Fund'. This fund was donated by the people of Surrey and managed by the town council under the direction of Sir John Jarvis, who came to Jarrow during the dark days of the 1930s with the £50,000 gift. Initially the donation was to assist the more needy cases in Northeast England, but during these troubled times, the plight of Jarrow was thought to be of greater importance than the rest of the region. Sir John came to Jarrow offering hope to its people, and a chance for them to get back on their feet with the promise of employment after the town was devastated at the closure of Palmer's.

Queen's Road

The first sod was cut for council housing in 1920, with the first house being occupied by the following year. From then until the cessation of building in 1940 because of the war, 1740 houses were provided at primrose at a cost of £890, 000. Building restarted in 1945, and in 1963 the council celebrated the opening of the 5,000th house. The next target on the council's programme was the demolition and rebuilding of properties in the Queen's Road area (pictured). At this time during the 1950s, when the photograph was taken most of the accommodation in the town centre was in a very bad state of repair and infestations of vermin and overcrowded conditions were also not uncommon. Many of the properties were blighted with severe dampness which was largely responsible for the poor state of health of many of the occupants. As the building programme gathered momentum, the housing in Palmer Street and surrounding area, were to be demolished and replaced with modern style housing.

Pearson Place

This was the site of the Alfred Pit dating from 1803. The photograph was taken from Pearson Place. To the right we see St Peter's church hall, and close to the centre is the Prince of Wales public house, which was demolished shortly after the photograph was taken in 1950, and replaced in 1958 on spare ground at the top of York Avenue. The white building to the left is the Golden Fleece in Commercial Road, one of two public houses with the same name, the other being close by in Ferry Street.

Tyne Tunnel Construction

Around 1950, Jarrow was recovering from the effects of the war, and the need for accommodation had never been greater. Part of this land was given over to new housing, and some years later the remainder was used for the construction of a ventilator for the forthcoming Tyne Tunnel. To the left of this 1960s photograph we see St Peter's church hall just prior to its demolition. Recently the area was landscaped after much activity during the construction of a sister tunnel.

Ferry Street

The skyline of many towns and cities up and down the country were often interrupted by the appearance of an eyesore commonly termed a gasometer, which incidentally was not a meter but a storage tank, or gasholder to give it its official name. It was William Murdoch who termed it a gasometer after he invented gas lighting for our homes and thoroughfares in the early nineteenth century. These storage tanks started to appear during the following years and were used until recently, supplying the nation with gas when most houses were illuminated and heated with this type of fuel. In some rare cases, it was necessary to conceal these tanks with brick work structures resembling buildings. Our own particular eyesore in Curlew Road, though no longer used, but remains a blot on the landscape These two contrasting images were taken from Ferry Street sixty years apart in 1953 and again in 2013.

Arndale Centre

As phase two of the shopping centre opened in the latter half of 1961, shops seemed to be springing up virtually overnight. Many new businesses were created at the advent of the centre, which attracted thousands of shoppers to Jarrow from around the region to see the traffic free precincts. The Arndale Property Trust who built the centre, were busy in other towns countrywide building similar precincts which were designed on a modern version of the more traditional market place. These motor-car- friendly centres were originally developed during the 1920s, and were to correspond to the rise of suburban living in many parts of the western world. Many of the High Street giants were attracted to the centres, and smaller businesses felt the benefit from their presence.

Etal Crescent

Public housing or council houses as they are more commonly known, was a way of providing affordable accommodation, but strict rules and criteria were applied for their allocation. Mass council house building commenced around 1920, for the sole purpose of replacing older dilapidated and irreparable properties nationwide. The Borough of Jarrow Councils contribution to this cause began in 1920 with the construction of houses at Monkton, and continued with various developments at an accelerated pace at Primrose, from around 1925, thus replacing many unfit dwellings in and around the town centre. These houses at Etal Crescent, Low Simonside are a prime example of the style of housing the council were providing between 1920 and 1950.

Grange Road

The appearance of high rise tower blocks in many towns and cities came about in this country after the second war as towns became suffocated with housing estates. Together with the ever rising price, and shortage of valuable land, especially in the south of the country, tower blocks were thought of as a quick fix solution. But it wasn't until 1963 when three smart and sought after tower blocks were built in Jarrow; Ellen, Wilkinson and Monastery Courts. Sadly quite a number of these towers became targets for vandalism and as a consequence were demolished. However, Jarrow escaped this wanton vandalism, the fifty-year-old towers, after recent refurbishment; remain as good as the day they were built. The 'right to buy' came about in 1979 when it gave sitting council tenants the opportunity to purchase the property at a discounted rate.

Back St Paul's Road

Terraced housing is a style of medium density housing which has been built in this country since the sixteenth century. Up market examples of this type of housing can be seen at Bath at Royal Crescent and Park Crescent London. Many rows of terraced houses were built in Jarrow in the second half of the nineteenth century, and provided reasonably priced accommodation for hundreds of families, similar to these in St Paul's Road. The first and last of these houses were called an end terrace and were often larger than the houses in the middle of the row. The waste ground at the bottom of the older of these two photographs from 1949, was the 'salt grass' for it was here harvested salt was laid to dry in the seventeenth century, in one of the town's lesser-known industries.

Ormonde Street

Tram systems were common throughout industrialised Britain in the nineteenth and twentieth centuries; almost all had disappeared by the 1950s. This occurred in Jarrow in 1929 when the service saw the end of its dominance in public transportation in favour of the motor bus. The system operated through our streets from 1906 to 1929. The electrically operated service was powered by overhead cables via a powerhouse in Beech Street, after the demise of the service the former power house was converted into the co-operative dairy in 1932. In recent years the tramcar has made a comeback in many of our major cities but more of a tourist attraction rather than a reliable transport service. The accompanying image from 1905 shows another section of track being laid in Ormonde Street.

Albert Road

For several years Jarrow has had an abundance of corner shops. Practically every street in the town centre had its own little emporium where you could purchase anything from a gas mantle to a clay pipe. Many of these often called gossip shops were open until very late at night prior to local licensing laws. Although convenience stores carry a larger range of goods, as their prices are often higher than the supermarkets they often struggle to remain open. The quaint little corner shop as we knew it similar to Christison's pictured on the corner of William Street and Albert Road have almost disappeared along with the family grocer. The corresponding image reveals this former busy thoroughfare is now a housing estate.

Monkton Road

A somewhat awkward looking yet elaborate little structure sat for many years at the junction of Monkton Road and High Street. Anyone born prior to 1960 will instantly recognise the building as a public convenience. Quite close to this building was a simple wooden structure known as 'the old man's shed' which was originally used by retired men who would meet here daily, stoke up their pipes and reminisce. These buildings were demolished around 1962. Today the area is occupied by a filling station.

Albion Street

This back yard in Albion Street is further evidence of the housing problem some endured within the town centre during the twenties and thirties. The stairway to the upper flat was removed due to it being in a dangerous condition, a direct result of neglect and the lack of maintenance this was replaced with a makeshift ladder. Geese and chickens roamed freely scratching for scraps of food. They were reared for the eggs they provided which were in extremely short supply commercially at this time. Almost every home in Jarrow had a cat or a dog which helped combat the vermin problem. Albion Street was demolished around 1945 and replaced with the Festival Flats in 1951, these were demolished in 1982. Today the area is a car park.

Jarrow Instruction Centre

Unemployed shipyard workers at the Jarrow Instruction Centre (JIC) which was located in the disused paper mill in Springwell Road fashioning the commemorative 'Bede Table'. The timber used for the solid oak table was donated by the Dean of Westminster, Reverend Prebend Austin Thompson. The completed table was to bear his coat of arms and St Paul's crest with the Latin inscription 'Sanctus Paulus'. The table has been in use for almost eighty years at St Paul's church (pictured). Various items of furniture were made by these talented men, who had recently acquired carpentry and cabinet making skills, for use in the Palmer Hospital, some of which were sold for a profit with the proceeds going towards the welfare of the centre and hospital.

Monkton Terrace

Monkton Terrace showing the bridge spanning the Newcastle to South Shields railway line. Whilst the bridge remains much the same today as it did when it was built, with the exception of the addition of a walkway behind the billboards visible either side of the road. Prior to this addition, pedestrians were expected to cross the bridge via the road. Increasing traffic levels forced the council to look at the situation in more detail, and declared the practice too dangerous to continue, and as a result the bill boards were removed and a safe walkway was constructed. The cottages to the left of this 1940 image were demolished some time later and replaced with housing and sheltered accommodation.

St Paul's Church

Part of the town's rich tapestry in former years were the street noises which echoed through the town but sadly have all but disappeared. The thunderous racket made by enormous road rollers, and the deafening sound of steel on steel as the trams wound their way along the busy streets. 'Hold tight!' hailed the tram driver. 'Rags and woollens!' called the totters. 'Calla herring!' sang out the womenfolk selling fish from a bucket from dawn until dusk. Another familiar echo from yesteryear was the newspaper vendor, when three editions of the *Jarrow Express* were printed daily. Churchgoers complained bitterly at this distraction during Sunday morning worship.

Co-op Offices

There is little photographic evidence of the rise of the Co-operative movement in Jarrow, but there is documentation stating a committee of the Jarrow Industrial Co-operative Society, comprising of fourteen businessmen who sat initially in January 1861. As a result of that meeting, the society opened its flagship shop in Commercial Road in March of the same year. Other outlets followed with the range of merchandise for sale increasing steadily. March 1892 saw the opening of a department store in North Street under the banner of the Jarrow & Hebburn Co-operative Society, tearooms and a restaurant followed nearby in Market Square. As the movement grew so did the need for a central office. In 1923, premises were built in Albert Road, which also housed the society's savings bank, facilities for its members paying insurance premiums and to collect dividends owing them. The parish of St Bede purchased the building during the seventies, turning it into a parish centre and social club. Today the building has reverted back to offices. It now goes under the name of St Bede's Chambers.

Stead Street

Gas lamps, cobblestones and flagged pavements.. These streets, and row upon row of dimly lit terraced houses, were home to hundreds of families who made their living in one of the town's many industries when Jarrow prospered and industry enjoyed a boom time. Sadly, the rapid deterioration of these dwellings in Stead Street meant demolition was to be the only solution, leaving vast empty spaces with nothing more than the echo of neighbourly gossip and children playing in the back lanes. However, the rebuilding programme which followed, brought with it hundreds of desirable new homes. These two photographs typify the changes.

Clayton Street

Another example of terraced housing in the central area. This time the camera is looking up Clayton Street, at the grimy terraced houses, blackened with decades of sooty deposits from the many years of heavy industry. The blackened buildings reflected the prosperity of the town, when men worked twelve hour shifts seven days a week in the shipyards. However, just prior to the outbreak of the Second War in 1939, around the same time as this photograph was taken, unemployment was at its peak, not only in Jarrow but the majority of the country was suffering as the depression tightened its grip. In the foreground are the cobblestones of Western Road showing the remnants of the tramlines.

Market Square

This 1960 image of Market Square shows the Theatre Royal and the Co-op buildings in North Street. The theatre was built in 1850 and was demolished in 1962. Many tons of rubble resulted in its demolition which was utilised in the construction of the Lindisfarne roundabout at Primrose. Close to the Market Square was the Excelsior, a private club for retired gentleman, which eventually became the Labour Party headquarters. A compulsory purchase order of the premises forced the Labour movement to seek new headquarters in Park Road. Clearly visible to the left of the older of these images is Straker's family butcher, who would offer bargain parcels of meat on a Saturday evening in the days prior to refrigeration. The modern photograph was taken from exactly the same spot fifty-three years later, and bears no resemblance to its counterpart.

Ormonde Street

Half way down Ormonde Street close to Lipton's grocery was a simple arch giving access to the rear of the street. Here sat a little old lady selling articles of second hand clothing for a few coppers, barely making enough to make ends meet. She was there in all weather week in and week out for many many years. I recall her being there during the 1950s. At the other end of the short arch was a set of double gates, reputed to be the entrance to the original Jarrow Market, where many deals, good and bad, were made. The arch is just visible to the right of the older of these two images.

Western Road

Another wonderful photograph from mushroom farmer James Hunter Carr, who recorded the changing face of the town during the 1940s and '50s. This time we are in Western Road in 1955. Modern fireplaces, as they were called, were fashionable around this time, and Radiant were the sole provider around these parts. The days of black leading the range were coming to an end, as people looked forward to better times ahead with more modern appliances. When these properties were demolished Radiant moved their showroom to Grange Road, prior to moving again to the recently appointed Bede Industrial Estate. The property in Western Road was formerly owned by undertaker William Hedley and was eventually used by another of the town's undertakers Bill Burlison to garage his vehicles. It was Hedley who loaned his horses to the fire and ambulance services during the 1930s.

Staple Road

For the past century, Jarrow has had a small but prolific community of Italian families who settled here from southern Italy, making Jarrow their home. Fionda, Rea and Coletta were just some of the names Jarrow folk were becoming familiar with, and were to provide the town and its people with ice cream parlours and fish & chip shops. This photograph from 1952 is of my grandmother Rosa Risi's ice cream parlour in Staple Road. Because of the relationship between Germany and Italy during the second war, some businesses became targets for vandalism. On four occasions my grandmother replaced the windows of her premises and on the fifth she was advised to board them up. This, reluctantly she did, and they remained this way until the property was demolished in 1958. Similar misfortunes happened to other families who traded in the town.

Mercantile Dry Dock
Close to the Shell depot in the east end of the town was the Mercantile Dry Dock & Co., which commenced trading in 1885, providing work for thousands of men until its demise ninety-six years later in 1981. In the older of these two aerial images from 1957, we see three dry docks to the right, and evidence of a fourth under construction just below the storage tanks. Vessels lying along side waiting for a berth was a common site the full length of the industrial part of the River Tyne. Aerial photography is the perfect medium to witness the changing face of our rural landscape. It is only from this eye in the sky viewpoint we see just how imposing the oil storage depot really was in the '50s.

St Peter's Church

St Peter's Church was in Chaytor Street and was consecrated on 29 June 1881, by the Bishop of Durham. The building covered an area of 500 square yards with seating for 400 worshipers, and a spire 117 feet tall, the top of which was demolished by a stray barrage balloon which broke free from its moorings in a nearby gas works. There was a large attendance of local dignitaries and members of all denominations present at the inaugural service. The church was built and furnished courtesy of Mrs Drewett, wife of Ormonde Drewett who was born at Jarrow Hall in 1839. Between them they did so much for the town having a genuine interest in the needs of its people. The church was demolished in 1963, adding to the list of disappearing buildings around the town.

Tyne Tunnel

HRH Queen Elizabeth visited Jarrow in October 1967, with The Duke of Edinburgh and Sir Ralph Carr Ellison Lord Lieutenant of Northumberland on the occasion of the opening ceremony of the Tyne Tunnel. After many years of wrangling as to where the new Tyne crossing was to be located, the project finally got under way in 1960, at a cost of £8.5m with a further £3.5m in reserve for the construction of the approach roads and ancillaries. The 5,500 foot long tunnel was constructed in an atmosphere of compressed air which was a revolutionary idea in 1960. A toll was introduced to offset the many millions which had been spent on the project. The toll booths and the administration buildings were erected on the north side at Howdon. In 2012, the royal couple returned to the area for the occasion of the official opening of a sister tunnel.

Monkton Terrace

Matt Scott established his Cumberland dairy and temperance bar in 1879. Matt is pictured outside the dairy in Monkton Terrace in 1906 with his delivery men who delivered milk to all parts of the town by horse drawn carts and hand barrows. Although there were several dairies in Jarrow at that time vying for business, this was the only one offering fresh dairy produce, direct from farms in and around Durham. The name Cumberland Dairy was dropped in favour of Holycroft Dairy, a name by which it was known up until the premises were demolished around 1964. Today, the scene has completely changed as has the way we purchase our milk. Deliveries by horse-drawn cart were phased out by the end of the 1960s at the introduction of the milk float, today, most of which have all but disappeared from our streets.

Bede Burn Road

Captain Robinson's orchard in the centre of the older of these two images was raided on several occasions by adolescent youngsters during the 1950s. Cappy as he was affectionately known was a big man with only one arm. Because of his disability, he became quite reclusive at his home Westfield House close to Croft Terrace until his death in 1967. Sightings of him were quite rare, but in most cases it was to chase youngsters from his property. He was a man of great wealth owning much land and property including the playing fields used by Croft Terrace School. Captain Robinson held a prominent position in the Boy Scout movement for many years. Westfield House and the orchard have long since disappeared, and been replaced with private houses, Westfield Court.

Slag Heap

For many decades, waste material of enormous proportions straddled the borders of both Jarrow and Hebburn at Monkton. This blot on an otherwise flawless skyline, grew daily into something resembling a small mountain, courtesy of the Palmer Shipbuilding Empire. The enormity of this slagheap reflected the prosperity of the Palmer years. Removal of the eyesore provided employment for hundreds of men over a period in excess of twenty years, from the 1950s culminating in the late '70s. Thousands of tons of this dross were transported to the continent and used in motorway construction. During the war years, the molten waste material was removed in open topped steel containers during daylight hours via a rail link, as the glowing waste would have been visible at night, and it was thought, this could provoke an air attack from enemy bombers. No trace of the slag heap exists today.

Western Road

When the older of these two photographs was taken in 1950, some towns were released from the scourge of food rationing. For Jarrow though, it was not until 1954 when shelves once again groaned under the strain of a plentiful supply of comestibles. The Amos Hinton grocery business was founded modestly in 1871 in Middlesbrough, and eventually rose to ninety-two outlets. During the early 1950s a branch opened up in Western Road. The Argyle Group purchased the company in 1984, and was subsequently absorbed into the Presto supermarket chain. Household names such as Hanlon's, Duncan's and Hadrian Stores Ltd were to fall by the wayside as they were swallowed up by the multiples.

Jarvis Park

Jarrow was a crowded town in the 1930s, and the provision for open spaces was looked upon as a necessity. Monkton Dene was developed from a 20-acre site, and provided casual work for 1,000 unemployed men. In 1876, the West Park was created providing bowling greens, cricket and football pitches. 1912 saw the opening of the Drewett Playing Fields close to St Paul's church. Jarvis Park was created in 1935 with cash from the Surrey Fund and named in honour of Sir John Jarvis, who did so much for the welfare of the town. Today the parkland is maintained by South Tyneside Council to a high standard, but health and safety issues forced them to abandon the paddling pool. The park is more commonly known today as its more familiar name, Valley View Park.

LABORE ET SCIENTIA

JARROW

Coat of Arms

The Borough of Jarrow was disbanded in 1974 when it was swallowed up along with Hebburn Urban District Council and the Boldon's at the formation of South Tyneside Metropolitan Borough Council. As the memory of Jarrow's coat of arms fades into the history books, I have resurrected these two and not too dissimilar images. The first is from 1875, when the borough was established. The three crowns symbolise King Ecgfrid, who donated the land to Abbott Benedict for the sole purpose of building a monastery. The link with the Venerable Bede is depicted by the church and the fort symbolises the Roman Station which was built here by Agricola. The town's shipbuilding heritage is remembered with a three-masted vessel. In the later version from 1928, we see the dragon clutching the golden crescent was retained, as was the crown and the link with shipbuilding. The church was replaced with an open book, and finally the shape of the crest was simplified and streamlined. The motto *Labore et Scientia* remained the same.

LABORE · ET · SCIENTIA

Butchers Bridge Road

The lone cyclist in the older of these two photographs was taken by local historian James Hunter Carr in 1949, in what we know today as Butchers Bridge Road. Prior to this, the thoroughfare was known as the Lonnen. At this time, the parish of St Matthew had been established for fourteen years and church services were conducted in the central building in the photograph. This simple wooden structure was classrooms for the girls of St Bede's Central School, and when necessary, doubled as the church. The building in the centre was Belsfield House, a convent and the main body of the school. St Matthews's church as we know it today didn't make its appearance until 1958. From 1960, the house and out buildings were converted into a school for boys, when the girls were transferred to the newly appointed St Josephs school at Hebburn. All traces of Belsfield House and the playing fields close by have disappeared.

Bede Burn Road

For many years Bede Burn Road has remained largely unchanged. The handsome terraced houses look as good today as they did when first built over a century ago. The electoral role from 1920 reveals this picturesque terrace was built most definitely for the middle classes, with the community comprising of upstanding and well-to-do citizens of the town. A by-law passed by the town council prevented the sale of intoxicating liquor in this particular residential area, which would have been a deciding factor for potential purchasers of the properties. Many desirable detached residences in this charming thoroughfare should not be over looked. One of them, Fairholme to the right of the older image from 1900, was used for many years as a police hostel when Jarrow police station was being used by Durham County Constabulary for training.

Monkton Leek & Floral Society

Monkton Leek, Vegetable & Floral society was founded in 1863. Although the membership has fluctuated from time to time, the enthusiasm of its members has ensured that the society is by far the most popular in South Tyneside, and is jointly the oldest of its kind in the country. During the formation of the society, judging and viewing took place in the Robin Hood public house close by. Then the Lord Nelson Inn became host for the annual event and has remained so to the present. One member Les Power, exhibited an impressive 312 cubic inches at the 2012 show which earned him first prize, and a coveted world record. The popularity of the autumn show is evident by the huge crowds it attracts and in 2013, the society celebrated its 150th anniversary.

Cambrian Street

Slum clearance continued for many years after the war. Smart new houses, maisonettes and flats mushroomed from the ground just as quick as the decaying property was torn down. The Festival Flats in High Street were built between 1947 and 1951 in response to Jarrow's post war housing problem. The eighty-four luxury flats reflected the latest trend in medium density housing and were viewed as a desirable modern alternative to the Victorian terrace. Sadly the complex became a prime target for vandalism, and was subsequently demolished in 1982. The older of these images was photographed from Cambrian Street in 1953, and shows the remnants of the properties in Burn's Street and Gray Street.

Park Methodist Church
Saturday was usually the day set aside for a wedding. With the war barely over, and most everyday items in short supply as rationing was still in force, people did what they could with what the resources available to them. This evocative photograph from 1951 of the wedding of Jean and Winston Taylor at Park Methodist church shows the happy couple en route to their reception which was usually held in the church hall or a nearby schoolroom. Invited guests would feast on simple fayre such as ham salad, followed by sherry trifle. Sadly, the church was closed to the public in 2012. The building was purchased in 2013 deconsecrated, refurbished and is now an auction house.

Pit Heap

This 1954 photograph was taken from Pearson Place. It was this part of the town which was used by travelling showmen, making their way north for the annual gathering on the town moor in Newcastle. The city has played host to the biggest travelling show in the world since 1883. Held the first week in June, the race week jamboree draws fairground attractions from all around the country and Europe. After the event, the gathering dispersed with the showmen going their separate ways, earning a living when and where they could during the summer months. Often their return visit to Jarrow was for months rather than weeks, weather permitting, and it was to nearby St Peters school they turned to educate their offspring. In 2012 and because of the constant heavy rain the travelling show was a complete washout and had to be abandoned. Early in 2013, a decision was taken to axe the 130-year-old funfair for good, as the showman's guild and the city council could not agree over rent and pitch terms.

Tyne Pedestrian Tunnel

Plans were in place for a passenger and cyclist tunnel under the bed of the river since 1937, but the 1939-45 conflicts halted any further progress. However, on 4 June 1946, the Minister of Transport, Right Honourable Jeffery Barnes MP inaugurated the Tyne pedestrian tunnel. Work commenced at Jarrow and simultaneously at Howdon on the north bank. The work went well with the breakthrough being on target and ahead of schedule ninety feet below the river. Two tunnels each 300 yards in length were provided for pedestrians and cyclists, at a cost of £750,000. Entry and exit to and from the tunnels was via escalator, which at the time of construction were the longest moving staircases in the world at 186 feet in length. Elevators were provided for wheelchair users and perambulators.

Tyne Pedestrian Tunnel

The new Tyne crossing was opened on 24 July 1951, serving both sides of the river, and was used by 20,000 commuters per day going to and from work. Today the tunnel is greatly in need of refurbishment. On 20 May 2013, the sixty-two-year-old complex was closed to the public for major repairs. The machinery which provided the power to drive the wooden escalators was becoming almost impossible to repair, two of which are about to be replaced with slanted elevators, similar to the principal of a funicular railway. The £4.5m refurbishment by the Tyne & Wear Integrated Transport Authority will be ready once again to serve commuters both sides of the river in 2014. The Grade II listed building stands as both a monument and testament to the men who built it, under the difficult and revolutionary methods adopted in its original construction.

Albert Road

This photograph taken at the foot of Albert Road during the summer of 1928 shows the aftermath of a hailstorm which lasted just ten minutes. Hailstones resembling golf balls fell from the sky, breaking windows and causing extensive damage to roofing and chimneys. Upon contact with the ground the hail fused together creating huge blocks of ice, making conditions hazardous for horse-drawn vehicles and pedestrians. The floods which followed, caused by the rapidly thawing ice, brought further problems. Many elderly people were confined to their homes as the council repaired the damage. This part of Albert Road no longer exists, which is evident in the more modern of these two contrasting images. However the railway bridge spanning it survives and carries the metro from Newcastle to South Shields.

Church Bank

The traditional Mayor Sunday procession commenced from the Town Hall, through the streets of Jarrow. Here is the Mayor Councillor Ralph C. Sparks in 1965 in full Mayoral regalia with the town clerk Gerald T. Noon and civic dignitaries on church bank *en route* to St Paul's church for a thanksgiving service. Musical accompaniment on such occasions was usually provided by the bands of the sea cadets, territorial and salvation armies. The building to the left is the former Jarrow Hall overlooking the Drewett playing fields, which were donated to the town by Henry Alfred Chaytor, the adopted son of Drewett Ormonde Drewett, who passed away in 1910. The council accepted the donation of the field, and in 1912, the recreational fields were officially opened to the public. Charles Harrison was appointed park keeper, to maintain the standards lay down by Chaytor, and from the then it became known as Charlie's Park.

Golden Lion

Of the fifty-four public houses in the town centre in 1922, only seven remain. The Golden Lion at the foot of Walter Street has survived as one of them. The accompanying image from 1932 shows the ornate facia of the building. Many landlords at the time organised brake and charabanc trips for their regulars to the seaside. South Shields and Seaburn were the usual venues for such outings. More than one hundred were recorded one day as the horse-drawn carriages from around the region trundled their way along the cobbled streets during the summer months for a picnic on the beach. Long gone is the ornate wooden facia and the charabanc, but the Golden Lion survived where others failed, along with the Ben Lomond, Royal Oak, Queens's arms, Crown and Anchor, Jarrow Crusaders and the Alexandra.

Mechanics Institute

Another of the town's memorable buildings was the Mechanics' Institute in Ellison Street. The building was a gift from the first mayor of Jarrow, Charles Mark Palmer in 1877, on the occasion of his second marriage to Gertrude Montgomery. The building was designed for social gatherings and reading rooms complete with a comprehensive library. During the 1950s, under the direction of the council, it was renovated and renamed the Civic Hall, and used as a venue for wedding receptions and similar functions. In recent years the Victorian structure was deemed unsafe and for some considerable time its future hung in the balance. After urgent remedial work the cosseted building was declared safe. The current proprietor restored the former institute to a very high standard, saving it once again from demolition, and providing the town with a restaurant, gymnasium and recreational facilities.

Pitt Street

Pitt Street was situated between Buddle Street and Commercial Road. The building to the left of this 1945 photograph was the rag shop, where members of the public could sell unwanted clothing for a few coppers to the owner Johnny Devlin who owned the premises from 1920 to 1955. William Towb purchased the business from Devlin and renamed it the Jarrow Iron & Metal Co., but the name rag shop stuck until the business finally closed in 1962. Totters came from far and wide to bargain with the terrible Towb in order to get the best possible price for their day's collection of old clothing, worn out mangles and all manner of ironmongery. In the centre of the photograph are the terraced houses in Buddle Street. None of these buildings survived beyond 1963 and the modern image reveals the area is now parkland.

Tyne Street

Another photograph taken by James Hunter Carr, this time in Tyne Street in 1948. The house to the left of the photograph was Hunter Carr's residence. He recorded the changing face of the town during the 1940s and '50s. It was my good fortune to inherit his voluminous collection of negatives along with the prints he made from them, and detailed descriptions. It was from this house he cultivated mushrooms and sold them in order to make a living. He also wrote music and played several instruments, he was also instrumental in the invention of RADAR. The genius also developed a method of producing perfume from whale oil. With the exception of his legacy of photographs, nothing survives from his property. When the building was demolished in the late 1950s he became resident of the Kent Hotel in Jesmond, Newcastle until his passing in 1964.

Town Hall

On 4 June 1875, Her Majesty Queen Victoria bestowed upon the town by charter the enviable status of Municipal Borough. This was closely followed by the election of councillors three months later on 10 August. The town was divided into four wards, with the appropriate number of councillors being elected for each. The swearing in took place in the boardroom of the Board of Health offices in Grange Road. Having elected the town's councillors and aldermen, the next important task was to elect the first mayor. Alderman Richardson moved the position be bestowed upon the founder of modern Jarrow, Charles Mark Palmer. This image from 1951 shows a large crowd gathering to witness the unveiling of the recently acquired town hall clock, purchased with the balance of the Surrey fund.

Retiring Council

The following November, Palmer resigned from the position. He informed the council of his decision to step down due to his business interests, and regrettably could not give the role of mayor his full commitment. Alderman Thomas Sheldon was entrusted with the mayoral duties having deputised for the former mayor on several occasions. The town hall was built, and opened in 1902, and it was from these corridors of power all council business was to take place until local government reorganisation in 1974. Pictured, the last mayor of Jarrow Councillor Vera Davison and members of the council at the time of local reorganisation 1973-74. Forty years on, the modern image reveals the former Council Chambers remain exactly as they did when the town hall was officially opened.

Monkton Terrace

Men women and children lined the streets in their hundreds, amid bunting and decorations to see a procession through the streets of Jarrow, en route to the Drewett playing fields for a thanksgiving open air mass to mark the 1,200th anniversary of the death of the Venerable Bede. The service on 12 June 1935 was celebrated by Archbishop of Westminster Arthur Hinsley, who later became Cardinal Hinsley, was assisted by Bishops from all parts of the British Isles and preached to the 50,000 pilgrims who came to pay homage to our patron saint. These photographs show the children from St Bede's school, in Monkton Road in procession to the Drewett playing fields for the ceremony, and what the area looks like today.

St Paul's Monastery Ruins

'I have spent my whole life in the same monastery, and while attentive to the rule of my order, and the service of the church, my constant pleasure lay in learning, teaching and writing.' These words were said by Bede in the monastery he loved at Jarrow, which he entered on AD 685 aged twelve years, and left only on his death in May AD 735. Although it probably had a Roman occupation the name Jarrow is derived from the Saxon word Gyrwe, roughly translated means marsh. It was also referred to as Jarrois in a seventeenth century print of the old church; the town as it was then, with a population of around 1400 was invaded by the Dane's in 794 and again in 866.

St Paul's Church

In 1070, an army of William the Conqueror destroyed the original monastery by fire. It was rebuilt in 1075 but alas dissolved in 1540, and its ruins have lain undisturbed close to St Paul's church at the mouth of the River Tyne for over 500 years. The chancel of the church was founded in the year 681 prior to the arrival of Bede. The basilica didn't make an appearance until much later, and for many years were two separate structures and not joined until 685 with the tower as we know it today. At this time the population was few and poor, consisting mainly of farmers and fishermen. This would account for the poor state of the church structure which became unsafe and as a consequence had to be demolished. This resulted in a poor substitute being built in 1782; in 1866 the present nave of the church was founded together with the north aisle.

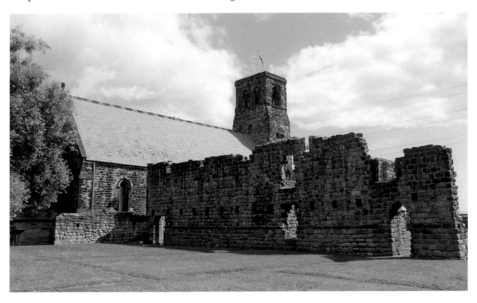

Bede's Well

The ancient spring of St Bede at Monkton,is more commonly known as Bedeswell. In the northern counties of England, many ancient wells and springs still exist. Some of these watering holes possess a legendary interest, having been associated with peculiar customs and ceremonies from centuries ago. As late as 1740, it was customary to bring children who were troubled with disease to Monkton, when a crooked pin was dropped into the well to experience the powers of the magic water. In 1908, Monkton Parish Council took steps towards the preservation of the well, and raised £200 in the belief that neighbouring Jarrow would destroy the ancient watering place. Although the well existed at the time of Bede, it is most unlikely he knew of its very existence, as the River Don which flows past the monastery ruins was once a crystal clear stream with fresh water and it is thought the monks used this as their water source.

St Bede's Church

It was Father Edmund Joseph Kelly who founded the parish of St Bede in Jarrow. He travelled daily to Jarrow from his parish in South Shields often on horseback, in atrocious weather conditions to celebrate mass at a house in High Street for anyone wishing to attend. Jarrow was a growing town at this time with a population of 3,500, with industry forming the backbone and structure of the town. Fr Kelly sought a site to build his church but after much wrangling with the site owner Drewett Brown it took four years to lay the foundations of the church. Contractors Lumsden and Mc Glinshey brought to the attention of Fr Kelly a clause in the lease, which stated 'no religious services or similar activity were to be performed within the boundaries of the site'.

St Bede's Choir

Six months went by before Drewett Brown relented. The contractors acting on behalf of Fr Kelly's instructions continued with the construction of the church. Fr Kelly and fellow priest Fr George Meynell, who incidentally was to be the first incumbent of the new church, toiled relentlessly with the men of the recently formed parish, and the Irish settlers who between them offered free labour. It was around this time Jarrow became known as little Ireland, as the small army of migrants from the Emerald Isle made Jarrow their home. The ceremony of laying the dedication stone was performed by the Bishop of Durham William Hogarth when he dedicated the 600-seat church to St Bede on 30 October 1860. The church was consecrated on 27 December 1861 at a concelebrated mass with Frs Kelly and Meynell along with visiting clergy. Pictured, the choir in 1967 and the altar as it is today.

St Bede's School

During the early part of the nineteenth century providing school buildings was a problem for the education authority. Private house schools were created for small groups of children around Caledonian Road, or at the Salem mission hall in High Street, which was operated by the Mormon fraternity. The Bede Parochial school was erected close to St Paul's church, and was set up by Measses chemical works which dominated the area for a number of years. The school was specifically used for the education of children of its employees. St Bede's first school came along in 1868; the one-roomed school was accessed by an entrance in Chapel Road (pictured). Records reveal there were five groups of desks, a blackboard and easel, and an assortment of second-hand books and slates. In 1870 the school was extended to accommodate more children, with a further entrance in Monkton Road.

East Jarrow School

In 1872, another one roomed school was provided at Low Jarrow, two years after the education act was implemented. Bertram Edwards was appointed head teacher in 1873, but retired three years later in 1876. From this time the school was used solely for the education of senior boys, with the girls continuing their education in the recently acquired extension of the Chapel Road School. Education was now organised and gathering momentum at this time, and was to see the arrival of an order of monks, the Marist Brothers, who specialised in teaching. The first to take the position of headmaster was Brother Valens, in 1876, and was succeeded by Brother Alban in 1879.

East Jarrow School

In 1906, the education committee had studied a report from HM Inspector of Schools which stated, 'The present head teacher, one of the Brothers, was under-qualified to continue with his role at the school, and did not meet the criteria laid down by HM Inspectors'. As a consequence the Marists were systematically removed from the school and after thirty years were replaced with trained certificated teachers with a minimum of two years' college training. St Bede's school in Harold Street became available in 1914.

Dedication Stone

St Paul's church on the north bank of the River Don dates from the seventh century, and holds the privilege of being one of the country's oldest buildings. This we can ascertain from two stones found in the church in 1782, which dedicates the church to St Paul on the *9th Kalends of May in the 15th year of King Egfriths reign*. These relics which commemorate this historic milestone have been preserved and are situated above the chancel arch. It has been claimed for many centuries that Jarrow was the site of a Roman Station, fort and village, and at the same time disclaimed by historians throughout history. However, it is believed the discoveries of two Roman inscriptions recovered during church renovations are indeed genuine. This claim is supported by a further discovery of two square pavements made from Roman brick, and with the style of Roman masonry, dating from the year 80 AD.

Springwell Paper Mill

The frequency and ferocity of localised fires especially in the farming community prompted a meeting of the Monkton Parish Council with a view to purchasing fire fighting equipment. Tenders were submitted with one for £72 being accepted. The breakdown reads: £53 for the appliance, £15 for the hose and reel, with a further £4 for shafts to harness the horse to. Springwell paper mill was forever suspect to outbreaks of fire due to the enormous amount of esparto grass stored here, which was a vital component in the manufacture of paper. In 1898 at Grange Farm, Monkton twelve or more haystacks caught fire. Tenders from Palmer's yard, Gateshead and Jarrow attended the scene, but due to the inefficient water supply, their efforts were all in vain. Pictured are the paper mill and the houses of Mill Dene View which replaced it.

West Park

Due to the lack of facilities, participants of green bowling were forced to carry out their pastime any way they could, relying on greens in other parks out of town on which to play their fixtures. Jarrow's own bowling green was opened by the mayor Thomas Renton just prior to the summer bowling season of 1894 in the spacious West Park. Various other sporting outdoor pursuits, depending on their size were held at the Metupa sports ground at Monkton. These facilities were given over to the town by the three major employers namely the Metals, Tube Works & Palmers, and it was from these three companies the word Metupa was derived. The venue was the perfect setting for the first Jarrow & District Floral & Horticultural Society gala. The two-day event attracted many visitors from the town and interested parties from as far afield as Durham and Darlington. The older of these images of the bowling greens at West Park dates from 1921.